jolly stuff

Dear Santa,

You know I love everything about you. I mean, you're so good to my kids, and nobody can wear red like you do! That's why I want you to know ahead of time that things will be different at my house this year.

I'm changing the way I'm decorating this Christmas. The whole traditional look—it's just got to go. I want to be surrounded by fresh fabrics in contemporary colors! That's why I'm sewing up this very cool collection of ornaments, tags, a banner, pillow, tree skirt, stockings, and table décor. The unexpected hues and fast appliqués are just so much fun!

But don't worry, SC. The cookies and cocoa will still be waiting for you on the dining table. That's never going to change.

By the way, how do you feel about aqua-striped placemats?

Hugs to you and Mrs. C.,
The Modern Crafter

LEISURE ARTS, INC.
Little Rock, Arkansas

peace quilt

Finished Size: 43" x 56" (109 cm x 142 cm)

yardage requirements

Yardage is based on 43"/44" (109 cm/112 cm) wide fabric.

- 2 yds (1.8 m) **total** of approximately 10 assorted green print fabrics
- 3/8 yd (34 cm) of red print fabric
- 3 1/8 yds (2.9 m) of fabric for backing
- 1/2 yd (46 cm) of fabric for binding

You will also need:

- 51" x 64" (130 cm x 163 cm) rectangle of batting
- Paper-backed fusible web
- Stabilizer

Instructions on page 20.

Peace

table runner

Finished Size: 12$^{1}/_{2}$" x 38$^{1}/_{2}$" (32 cm x 98 cm)

yardage requirements

Yardage is based on 43"/44" (109 cm/112 cm) wide fabric.

$^{1}/_{2}$ yd (46 cm) of red print fabric
$^{1}/_{4}$ yd (23 cm) of multi-color stripe fabric
Eleven squares 4$^{1}/_{2}$" x 4$^{1}/_{2}$" (11 cm x 11 cm) of assorted print fabrics
$^{1}/_{2}$ yd (46 cm) of fabric for backing

You will also need:

15" x 41" (38 cm x 104 cm) rectangle of batting
Template plastic

Instructions on page 22.

placemat

Finished Size: $18^1/_4$" x $12^1/_2$" (46 cm x 32 cm)

yardage requirements

Yardage is based on 43"/44" (109 cm/112 cm) wide fabric and is for making one placemat.

$^1/_2$ yd (46 cm) of dark green print fabric
$^1/_4$ yd (23 cm) of light green print fabric
$^1/_8$ yd (11 cm) of multi-color stripe fabric
Scrap of fabric for appliqué
$^1/_2$ yd (46 cm) of fabric for backing

You will also need:

$19^1/_4$" x $13^1/_2$" (49 cm x 34 cm) rectangle of batting
Paper-backed fusible web
Stabilizer

Instructions on page 23.

Claire

tree skirt

Finished Size: 39" x 39" (99 cm x 99 cm)

yardage requirements

Yardage is based on 43"/44" (109 cm/112 cm) wide (or wider) fabric.

- $1^1/_4$ yds (1.1 m) of red felt
- $^1/_2$ yd (46 cm) of black and white print fabric for binding
- $1^1/_4$ yds (1.1 m) of fabric for backing

You will also need:

- White embroidery floss
- Tracing paper

Instructions on page 24.

joy
noel

stockings

Yardage is based on 43"/44" (109 cm/112 cm) wide fabric.

flower stocking yardage requirements

5/8 yd (57 cm) of red print fabric
1/2 yd (46 cm) of purple print fabric
Scraps of green and yellow print fabrics
5/8 yd (57 cm) of fabric for lining
8" (20 cm) of 3/8" (10 mm) wide ribbon
Two 14" x 22" (36 cm x 56 cm) rectangles of batting
Paper-backed fusible web
Stabilizer

Instructions on page 25.

ruched stocking yardage requirements

1/2 yd (46 cm) of pink print fabric
1/4 yd (23 cm) of brown print fabric
1/2 yd (46 cm) of muslin
5/8 yd (57 cm) of fabric for lining
8" (20 cm) of 3/8" (10 mm) wide ribbon
Two 14" x 22" (36 cm x 56 cm) rectangles of batting

Instructions on page 26.

dove stocking yardage requirements

1/2 yd (46 cm) of blue print fabric
1/4 yd (23 cm) of red print fabric
1/4 yd (23 cm) of white solid fabric
5/8 yd (57 cm) of fabric for lining
8" (20 cm) of 3/8" (10 mm) wide ribbon
Two 14" x 22" (36 cm x 56 cm) rectangles of batting
Paper-backed fusible web
Stabilizer

Instructions on page 28.

joy banner

Finished Size: approximately 40" (102 cm) wide

yardage requirements

Yardage is based on 43"/44" (109 cm/112 cm) wide fabric.

1/8 yd (11 cm) of red dot print fabric
1/4 yd (23 cm) of red stripe fabric
1/4 yd (23 cm) each of green, yellow, and blue print fabrics
Scraps of assorted red/fuchsia print fabrics for appliqués

You will also need:

Paper-backed fusible web
Stabilizer

Instructions on page 30.

tags

reindeer tag supplies

Scraps of red, green and white print fabrics
7" (18 cm) of 5/8" (16 mm) wide ribbon
6" x 4" (15 cm x 10 cm) rectangle of Pellon® Peltex 70 sew-in interfacing
Paper-backed fusible web
Stabilizer

Instructions on page 31.

flower tag supplies

Scraps of white, red and yellow print fabrics
7" (18 cm) of 5/8" (16 mm) wide ribbon
5" x 5" (13 cm x 13 cm) square of Pellon® Peltex 70 sew-in interfacing
1 1/8" (29 mm) diameter button
Paper-backed fusible web
Stabilizer

Instructions on page 32.

reindeer pillow

Finished Size: 20" x $15^1/_2$" (51 cm x 39 cm)

yardage requirements

Yardage is based on 43"/44" (109 cm/112 cm) wide fabric.

8 strips 3" x 16" (8 cm x 41 cm) of assorted red print fabrics

10" x 10" (25 cm x 25 cm) piece of white solid fabric

$20^1/_2$" x 16" (52 cm x 41 cm) piece of fabric for pillow backing

You will also need:

Two $22^1/_2$" x 18" (57 cm x 46 cm) rectangles of batting

Polyester fiberfill

Paper-backed fusible web

Stabilizer

Instructions on page 33.

ornaments

owl ornament supplies

Scraps of yellow, purple, red, white, and brown felt
6" (15 cm) of 1/8" (3 mm) wide ribbon
9 mm sequins
Embroidery floss - blue, green, and yellow
Polyester fiberfill

Instructions on page 34.

flower ornament supplies

Scrap of light green felt
Scraps of red, yellow and fuchsia print fabrics
8" (20 cm) of 1/8" (3 mm) wide ribbon
Polyester fiberfill
Paper-backed fusible web
Stabilizer

Instructions on page 35.

dove ornament supplies

Scraps of red, yellow, and green felt
9" (23 cm) of 1/8" (3 mm) wide ribbon
Small yellow and green beads
Embroidery floss - green
Polyester fiberfill
Fabric glue

Instructions on page 35.

peace quilt

cutting out the pieces

*Follow **Rotary Cutting**, page 36, to cut fabric. Cut all strips across the selvage-to-selvage width of the fabric. All measurements include 1/4" seam allowances.*

From assorted green print fabrics:

- Cut **strips** 3 1/2" wide and random lengths.
- Cut **strips** 4 1/2" wide and random lengths.

From fabric for binding:

- Cut 6 **binding strips** 2 1/2" wide.

cutting the appliqués

*Follow **Preparing Fusible Appliqués**, page 38, to use patterns on insert. **Note:** Appliqué patterns are printed in reverse.*

From red print fabric:

- Cut **letters** P, E, A, C, and E.

assembling the quilt

*Follow **Sewing** and **Pressing**, page 37. Use a 1/4" seam allowance. Refer to **Quilt Top Diagram** for placement of strips and appliqués. Refer to **Satin Stitch Appliqué**, page 39, for technique.*

1. Lay **strips** end to end and side by side as shown in **Fig. 1**. The length of the strips should be random but when sewn the center of the quilt should be approximately 56" long.

Fig. 1

2. Sew strips together end to end.
3. Sew long edges of strips together.
4. Trim quilt top to 55" long.
5. Fuse **letters** to quilt top; satin stitch in place.
6. Follow **Quilting**, page 40, to mark, layer, and quilt as desired. Our quilt is machine quilted in the ditch along each strip and around each letter.
7. Refer to **Making A Hanging Sleeve**, page 43, to make and attach a hanging sleeve, if desired.
8. Follow **Binding**, page 43, to bind quilt.

Quilt Top Diagram

table runner

cutting the pieces

*Follow **Rotary Cutting**, page 36, to cut fabric. All measurements include 1/4" seam allowances.*

From red print fabric:

- Cut **table runner top** 14" x 40".

From multi-color stripe fabric:

- Cut 2 **ruffles** 4" x 23".

From fabric for backing:

- Cut **table runner back** 13" x 39".

cutting the appliqués

*Follow **Template Cutting**, page 37, to use pattern on insert. **Note:** Patterns do not include seam allowances.*

From assorted print fabrics:

- Cut 11 **hexagons**.

assembling the table runner

*Follow **Sewing** and **Pressing**, page 37. Use a 1/4" seam allowance. Follow **Needle-Turn Appliqué**, page 38.*

1. Beginning and ending 3/4" from end of **table runner top**, appliqué hexagons to table runner top.
2. Topstitch 1/8" inside each hexagon shape.
3. Center table runner top on batting.
4. Follow **Quilting**, page 40, to quilt table runner top and batting as desired. Our table runner is quilted with a meandering pattern over the top and in the ditch around the hexagons. Centering hexagons, trim top to 13" x 39".
5. Match right sides and raw edges and fold **ruffle** in half lengthwise. Sew along each short end. Turn ruffle right side out; press. Repeat for remaining ruffle.
6. Baste ruffles 1/4" and 1/8" from raw edges.
7. Beginning and ending 1/4" from edge of table runner, use basting stitches to gather 1 ruffle to fit 1 short edge; pin. Repeat for remaining ruffle. Adjusting gathers as necessary, baste ruffles in place 1/8" from raw edges.
8. Matching right sides, layer table runner top and **table runner back** with ruffle sandwiched in between. Stitch around all sides, leaving an opening for turning.
9. Turn table runner right side out, press, and stitch opening closed.
10. Starting and stopping at the hexagons, topstitch around all sides of table runner 1/4" from edges.

placemat

cutting the pieces

*Follow **Rotary Cutting**, page 36, to cut fabric. All measurements include 1/4" seam allowances.*

From dark green print fabric:

- Cut **large rectangle** 15" x 13".

From light green print fabric:

- Cut **small rectangle** 4 1/4" x 13".

From multi-color stripe fabric:

- Cut **ruffle** 2 1/2" x 21 1/2".

From fabric for backing:

- Cut **backing** 18 3/4" x 13".

cutting the appliqués

*Follow **Preparing Fusible Appliqués**, page 38, to use pattern on insert.*

***Note:** Appliqué pattern is printed in reverse.*

From scrap of fabric:

- Cut 1 **dove**.

assembling the placemat

*Follow **Sewing** and **Pressing**, page 37. Use a 1/4" seam allowance. Refer to **Satin Stitch Appliqué**, page 39, for technique.*

1. Match right sides and raw edges and fold **ruffle** in half lengthwise. Sew along each short end. Turn ruffle right side out; press.
2. Baste ruffle 1/4" and 1/8" from raw edges.
3. Beginning and ending 1/4" from edge of **large rectangle**, use basting stitches to gather ruffle to fit 1 short edge; pin. Adjusting gathers as necessary, baste ruffle in place 1/8" from raw edges.
4. To make placemat top, match right sides and sew **small rectangle** to large rectangle with ruffle sandwiched in between. Open and press ruffle towards small rectangle. Topstitch 1/8" from short edge of large rectangle near ruffle.
5. Fuse **dove** to placemat top; satin stitch in place.
6. Center placemat top on batting.
7. Keeping ruffle free, follow **Quilting**, page 40, to quilt placemat and batting as desired. Our placemat is quilted with meandering quilting over the top and in the ditch around the appliqué. Trim batting even with top.
8. Matching right sides, layer the placemat top and **backing**. Keeping ruffle free, stitch around all sides, leaving an opening for turning.
9. Turn placemat right sides out, press, and stitch opening closed.
10. Starting and stopping at ruffle, topstitch 1/4" from outer edges.

tree skirt

cutting the pieces

*Follow **Rotary Cutting**, page 36, to cut fabric. Cut all strips across the selvage-to-selvage width of the fabric. All measurements include 1/4" seam allowances.*

From red felt:

- Cut **square** 38 1/2" x 38 1/2".

From black and white print fabric:

- Cut 5 **binding strips** 2 1/2" wide.

From fabric for backing:

- Cut **backing** 38 1/2" x 38 1/2".

assembling the tree skirt

*Use a 1/4" seam allowance. Refer to **Tree Skirt Diagram** for embroidery placement.*

1. To make tree skirt top, measure 9" along 2 adjacent sides from corner of **square**. Mark at each point. Draw a line from each point (**Fig. 1**). Cut along drawn line. Repeat for each corner.
2. Fold tree skirt top in half in each direction to find center. Refer to **Fig. 2** to mark center opening 3 1/4" from corner. Cut along drawn line; unfold. For opening, fold tree skirt in half from 1 long edge to circle; cut along fold.
3. Follow **Transferring Embroidery Patterns**, page 45, to transfer words using patterns on insert. Follow **Hand Stitches**, page 46, to use 4 strands of floss to Backstitch words and snowflakes on tree skirt top. Straight Stitch centers of snowflakes.
4. Matching wrong sides, pin tree skirt top to **backing**. Trim backing around edges of tree skirt top, cutting along opening and center circle. Baste edges of top and backing together.
5. Follow **Binding**, page 43, to bind tree skirt.

Fig. 1

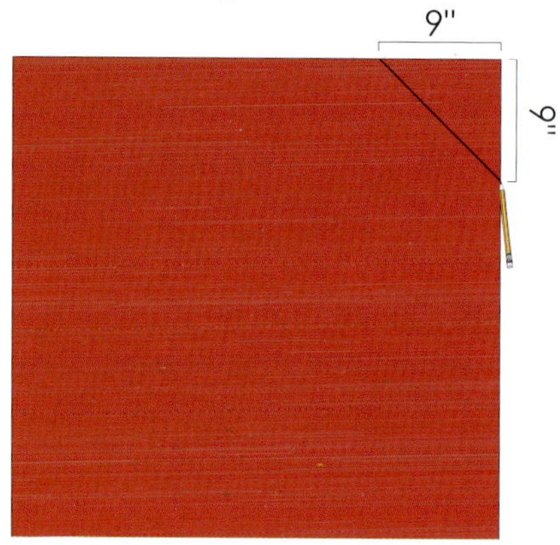

Fig. 2

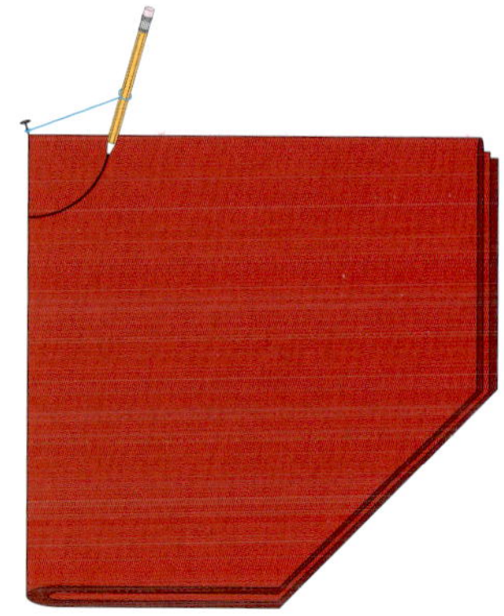

Tree Skirt Diagram

flower stocking

Finished Size: 12 1/2" x 19 1/2" (32 cm x 50 cm)

cutting the pieces

*Follow **Rotary Cutting**, page 36, to cut fabric. Use patterns on insert. All measurements include 1/4" seam allowances.*

From red print fabric:

- Cut 1 **stocking front**; cut 1 **stocking back** in reverse.

From purple print fabric:

- Cut **ruffle** 5 1/2" x 40".
- Cut **binding** 2 1/2" x 16 1/2".

From fabric for lining:

- Cut 1 **stocking front lining**; cut 1 **stocking back lining** in reverse.

cutting the appliqués

*Follow **Preparing Fusible Appliqués**, page 38, to use patterns on insert.* ***Note:*** *Appliqué patterns are printed in reverse.*

From green print fabric:

- Cut 3 **outer flowers**.

From purple print fabric:

- Cut 3 **inner flowers**.

From yellow print fabric:

- Cut 3 **flower centers**.

appliquéing the stocking

*Refer to **Satin Stitch Appliqué**, page 39, for technique.*

1. Fuse appliqués to **stocking front**. (***Note:*** *For flower on toe, arrange appliqués as desired, allowing some of the appliqué to hang off the edges of the stocking front. Before fusing, trim away the portion of the appliqué hanging off of stocking front.)*
2. Satin stitch pieces in place.

assembling the stocking

*Follow **Sewing** and **Pressing**, page 37. Use a 1/4" seam allowance.*

1. Layer batting on wrong side of stocking front. Layer batting on wrong side of **stocking back**.
2. Follow **Quilting**, page 40, to quilt stocking and batting as desired. Our stocking front is machine quilted in the ditch around each appliqué and the stocking front and back are machine quilted with meander quilting.
3. Layer stocking pieces as follows from bottom to top:
   stocking back, right side up
   stocking front, wrong side up
   stocking lining pieces, right sides facing
4. Leaving top edges open, sew layers together. Clip curves and turn stocking right side out. Sew lining to stocking around stocking opening.
5. Sew short ends of **ruffle** together. Matching wrong sides and raw edges, fold ruffle in half lengthwise; press. Baste 1/4" and 1/8" from raw edges. Gather ruffle to fit stocking opening; pin. Baste ruffle to stocking a scant 1/4" from stocking opening.
6. Follow **Binding**, page 43, to bind stocking opening.
7. Fold ribbon in half; knot ends together. Sew fold of ribbon inside stocking opening.

ruched stocking

Finished Size: 12½" x 19½" (32 cm x 50 cm)

cutting the pieces

*Follow **Rotary Cutting**, page 36, to cut fabric. Use pattern on insert. All measurements include ¼" seam allowances.*

From pink print fabric:

- Cut 1 **stocking front** (shorter shape); cut 1 **stocking back** in reverse (shorter shape).

From brown print fabric:

- Cut **ruching** 4¼" x 18".
- For cuff back, cut **cuff** in reverse.

From muslin:

- Cut 1 **stocking front** (longer shape).

From fabric for lining:

- Cut 1 **stocking lining front;** cut 1 **stocking lining back** in reverse (longer shape).

assembling the stocking

*Follow **Sewing** and **Pressing**, page 37. Use a ¼" seam allowance.*

1. Baste **ruching** ¼" and ⅛" from long raw edges. Matching right sides, gather ruching to fit top edge of **stocking front**; pin. Sew ruching to stocking front. Matching wrong side of stocking front/ruching to right side of muslin **stocking front**, gather ruching to fit muslin and baste pieces together.
2. Sew **cuff** to **stocking back**.
3. Topstitch on ruching and stocking front along seamline.

4. Layer batting on wrong side of stocking front. Layer batting on wrong side of stocking back.
5. Follow **Quilting**, page 40, to quilt stocking front and batting as desired. Our stocking front is machine quilted following the zigzag stripes of the fabric. Ruched cuff is not quilted. Quilt stocking back as desired. Our stocking back is machine quilted following the zigzag stripes of the fabric and the cuff back is meander quilted. Trim excess batting from stocking front and back.
6. Matching right sides, sew stocking front to **stocking lining front** along top edge. Repeat for stocking back and **stocking lining back**.
7. Matching right sides and leaving an opening for turning, sew stocking front/ lining to stocking back/lining along all edges (**Fig. 1**).
8. Turn stocking right side out; sew opening closed.
9. Insert lining into stocking; press. Topstitch $^{1}/_{4}$" from edge of stocking opening.
10. Fold ribbon in half; knot ends together. Sew fold of ribbon inside stocking opening.

Fig. 1

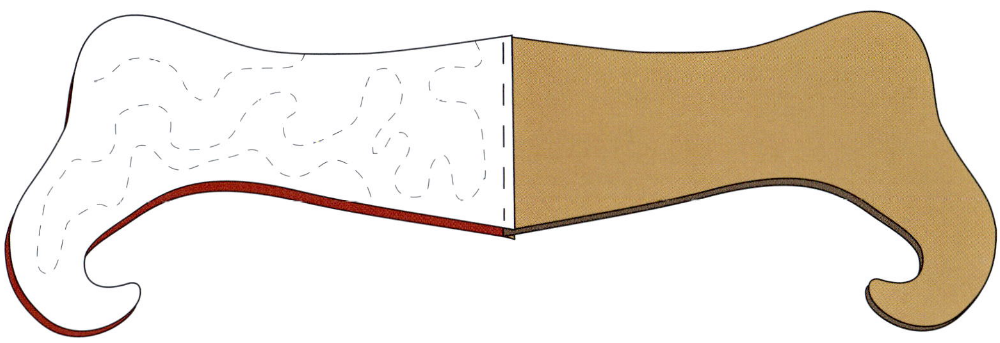

dove stocking

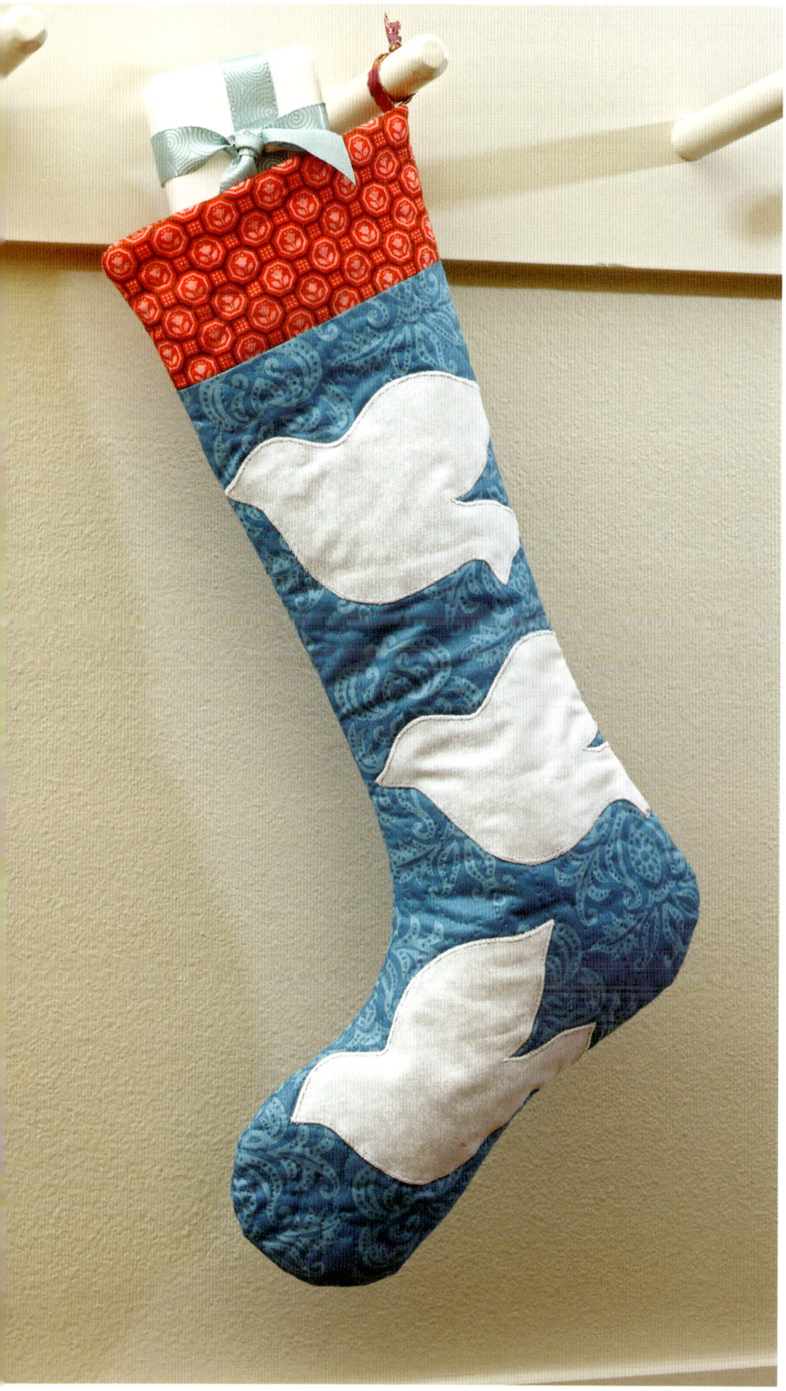

Finished Size: 12$^{1}/_{2}$" x 19$^{1}/_{2}$" (32 cm x 50 cm)

cutting the pieces

Use patterns on insert. All measurements include $^{1}/_{4}$" seam allowances.

From blue print fabric:

- Cut 1 **stocking front** (shorter shape); cut 1 **stocking back** in reverse (shorter shape).

From red print fabric:

- Cut **cuff**.
- For **cuff back**, cut cuff in reverse.

From fabric for lining:

- Cut 1 **stocking lining**; cut 1 **stocking lining** in reverse (longer shape).

cutting the appliqués

*Follow **Preparing Fusible Appliqués**, page 38, to use pattern on insert. **Note:** Appliqué pattern is printed in reverse.*

From white solid fabric:

- Cut 3 **doves**.

appliquéing the stocking

*Refer to **Satin Stitch Appliqué**, page 39, for technique.*

1. Fuse **doves** to **stocking front**. ***(Note:** Arrange appliqués as desired, allowing some of appliqué to hang off the edges of the stocking front. Before fusing, trim away the portion of appliqué hanging off of the stocking front.)*
2. Satin stitch doves in place.

assembling the stocking

*Follow **Sewing** and **Pressing**, page 37. Use a* $^{1}/_{4}$*" seam allowance.*

1. Matching right sides, sew **cuff** to **stocking front**. Matching right sides, sew **cuff back** to **stocking back**.
2. Layer batting on wrong side of **stocking front**. Layer batting on wrong side of **stocking back**.
3. Follow **Quilting**, page 40, to quilt stocking and batting as desired. Our stocking front is machine quilted in the ditch around each appliqué and the stocking front and back are machine quilted with meander quilting. Trim excess batting from stocking front and back.
4. Matching right sides and with toes facing same direction, sew stocking front to **stocking lining** along top edge. Repeat for stocking back and remaining stocking lining.
5. Matching right sides and leaving an opening for turning, sew stocking front/ lining to stocking back/lining along all edges (**Fig. 1**).
6. Turn stocking right side out; sew opening closed.
7. Insert lining into stocking; press.
8. Fold ribbon in half; knot ends together. Sew fold of ribbon inside stocking opening.

Fig. 1

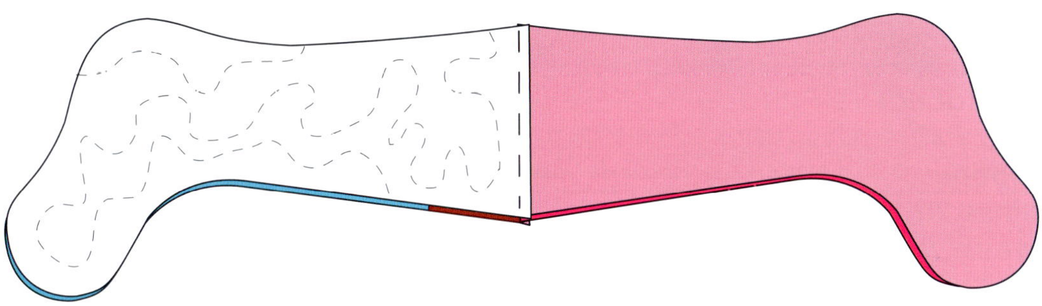

joy banner

cutting the pieces

Follow ***Rotary Cutting****, page 36, to cut fabric. Cut all strips across the selvage-to-selvage width of the fabric. Use pattern on insert. All measurements include $^1/_4$" seam allowances.*

From red dot print fabric:

- Cut **strip** 2" x 40".

From red stripe fabric:

- Cut 3 **ruffles** $2^1/_2$" x 34".

From *each* of green, yellow, and blue print fabrics:

- Cut 1 **background**; cut 1 **background lining**.

cutting the appliqués

Follow ***Preparing Fusible Appliqués****, page 38, to use patterns on insert.* ***Note:*** *Appliqué patterns are printed in reverse.*

From assorted red/fuchsia print fabrics:

- Cut **letters** J, O, and Y.

appliquéing the banner

Refer to ***Satin Stitch Appliqué****, page 39, for technique.*

1. Fuse **letter** to **background**.
2. Satin stitch letter to background.
3. Repeat Steps 1-2 for each background.

assembling the banner

Follow ***Sewing*** *and* ***Pressing****, page 37. Use a $^1/_4$" seam allowance.*

1. Matching wrong sides and raw edges, fold 1 **ruffle** in half lengthwise; press. Baste $^1/_4$" and $^1/_8$" from raw edges. Matching one side of ruffle to right side of 1 background, gather ruffle to fit background; pin. Baste ruffle to background.
2. Matching right sides and raw edges, pin background and **background lining** together with ruffle sandwiched in between.
3. Leaving top edges open, sew layers together around curved edge. Turn background right side out; press. Baste top edges closed.
4. Repeat Steps 1-3 for remaining backgrounds.
5. Matching wrong sides, press **strip** in half lengthwise; unfold. Press long raw edges to meet fold line. Refold strip; press.
6. Spacing the backgrounds as desired, place the top edges of the backgrounds inside the fold of the strip; pin. Topstitch along edge of strip, catching backgrounds in stitching as you sew. Knot ends of strip.

reindeer tag

Finished Size: 6" x 4" (15 cm x 10 cm)

cutting the pieces

*Follow **Rotary Cutting**, page 36, to cut fabric. All measurements include ¼" seam allowances.*

From red print fabric:

- Cut **large rectangle** 4¾" x 4".

From green print fabric:

- Cut **small rectangle** 1¾" x 4".

From scrap of fabric:

- Cut **backing** 6" x 4".

cutting the appliqués

*Follow **Preparing Fusible Appliqués**, page 38, to use pattern on insert.* ***Note:*** *Appliqué pattern is printed in reverse.*

From white print fabric:

- Cut **reindeer**.

assembling the tag front

*Follow **Sewing** and **Pressing**, page 37. Use a ¼" seam allowance.*

1. Sew **small rectangle** to one short edge of **large rectangle**.
2. Refer to **Fig. 1** to measure and mark points on top right corner of large rectangle. Cut from point to point. Repeat for bottom right corner.

Fig. 1

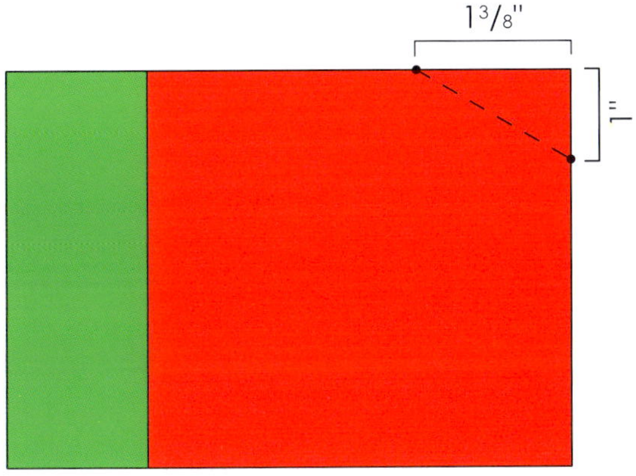

appliquéing the tag

*Refer to **Satin Stitch Appliqué**, page 39, for technique.*

1. Fuse **reindeer** to large rectangle.
2. Satin stitch reindeer to large rectangle.

assembling the tag

1. Layer tag front on top of interfacing and **backing**. Use tag front as a pattern to trim corners of interfacing and backing.
2. Fold ribbon in half. Place folded end between layers.
3. Sew layers together using a zigzag stitch around all edges, catching ribbon in stitching.
4. Trim ribbon ends as desired.
5. If desired, use rubber stamps and permanent ink to stamp To and From on back of tag. Use a permanent pen to write names.

flower tag

Finished Size: $4^1/_2$" (11 cm) diameter

cutting the pieces

Use pattern on insert.

From white print fabric:

- Cut **circle**.
- Cut **backing**.

From interfacing:

- Cut **circle**.

cutting the appliqués

*Follow **Preparing Fusible Appliqués**, page 38, to use patterns on insert.*

***Note:** Appliqué patterns are printed in reverse.*

From red print fabric:

- Cut **outer flower**.

From yellow print fabric:

- Cut **inner flower**.

appliquéing the tag

*Refer to **Satin Stitch Appliqué**, page 39, for technique.*

1. Fuse appliqués on **circle**.
2. Satin stitch pieces to circle.
3. Sew button to flower center.

assembling the tag

1. Layer circle on top of **interfacing circle** and **backing**.
2. Fold ribbon in half. Place folded end between layers.
3. Sew layers together using a zigzag stitch around edges, catching ribbon in stitching.
4. Trim ribbon ends as desired.
5. If desired, use rubber stamps and permanent ink to stamp To and From on back of tag. Use a permanent pen to write names.

reindeer pillow

cutting the appliqués

*Follow **Preparing Fusible Appliqués**, page 38, to use pattern on insert. **Note:** Appliqué pattern is printed in reverse.*

From white solid fabric:

- Cut 1 **reindeer**.

assembling the pillow

*Follow **Sewing** and **Pressing**, page 37. Use a 1/4" seam allowance. Refer to **Satin Stitch Appliqué**, page 39, for technique.*

1. To make pillow top, match long edges and sew **strips** together.
2. Fuse **reindeer** to pillow top; satin stitch in place.
3. Layer batting on wrong side of pillow top. Layer batting on wrong side of **pillow back**.
4. Follow **Quilting**, page 40, to quilt pillow front and batting as desired. Our pillow front is machine quilted in the ditch along each strip and around the appliqué. Quilt pillow back and batting as desired. Our pillow back is machine quilted with vertical lines spaced 2 1/2" apart. Trim batting even with pillow top and pillow back.
5. Matching right sides and leaving an opening for turning, sew pillow front and pillow back together. Turn pillow right side out.
6. Stuff pillow with fiberfill; sew opening closed.

owl ornament

Finished Size: 4½" x 5" (11 cm x 13 cm)

cutting the pieces

Use patterns on insert.

From yellow felt:

- Cut **front**.

From purple felt:

- Cut 2 **wings**.

From red felt:

- Cut **topknot**.

From white felt:

- Cut 2 **eyes**.

From brown felt:

- Cut **back**.
- Cut **beak**.

assembling the ornament

*Refer to **Hand Stitches**, page 46, and use 3 strands of floss unless otherwise indicated.*

1. Using blue floss and Straight Stitches, embroider **eyes**. Using green floss and Running Stitch, sew eyes to **front**. Using yellow floss and Straight Stitches, sew **beak** to front.
2. Using 1 strand of blue floss, sew sequins to the body (**Fig. 1**).

Fig. 1

3. Leaving the top edges open and using a zigzag stitch, sew front and **back** together along sides and bottom edges.
4. Stuff body with fiberfill.
5. Fold ribbon in half. Catching ribbon ends in stitching at center top, zigzag stitch opening closed.
6. *(**Note:** Where pieces extend beyond body, continue stitching Running Stitch.)* Using blue floss and a Running Stitch, sew **topknot** to body. Using yellow floss and a Running Stitch, sew **wings** to body.

flower ornament

Finished Size: 5" (13 cm)

cutting the pieces

Use patterns on insert.

From light green felt:

- Cut 2 **ornaments**.

cutting the appliqués

*Follow **Preparing Fusible Appliqués**, page 38, to use patterns on insert.*

***Note:** Appliqué patterns are printed in reverse.*

From red print fabric:

- Cut **outer flower**.

From yellow print fabric:

- Cut **inner flower**.

From fuchsia print fabric:

- Cut **flower center**.

appliquéing the tag

*Refer to **Satin Stitch Appliqué**, page 39, for technique.*

1. Fuse appliqués to one **ornament**.
2. Satin stitch appliqués to **ornament**.

assembling the tag

1. Leaving the top edges open and using a zigzag stitch, sew ornaments together around edges.
2. Stuff ornament with fiberfill.
3. Fold ribbon in half. Catching ribbon ends in stitching at center top, zigzag opening closed.

dove ornament

Finished Size: $6^1/_2$" x 4" (17 cm x 10 cm)

cutting the pieces

Use patterns on insert.

From red felt:

- Cut 2 **bodies**.

From yellow felt:

- Cut 2 **flowers**.

From green felt:

- Cut 4 **leaves**.

assembling the ornament

1. Glue 1 **flower** and 2 **leaves** to 1 **body**.
2. Using 3 strands of green floss, Running Stitch stems for flowers. Sew on beads for flower and eye.
3. Repeat Steps 1-2 with remaining pieces.
4. Leaving an opening along top edges for stuffing and using a zigzag stitch, sew bodies together.
5. Stuff body with fiberfill.
6. Fold ribbon in half. Catching ribbon ends in stitching at center top, zigzag stitch opening closed.

general instructions

To make your project easier and more enjoyable, we encourage you to carefully read all of the general instructions, study the color photographs, and familiarize yourself with the individual project instructions before beginning.

fabrics

selecting fabrics

Choose high-quality, medium-weight 100% cotton fabrics. All-cotton fabrics hold a crease better, fray less, and are easier to quilt than cotton/polyester blends.

Yardage requirements listed for each project are based on 43"/44" wide fabric with a "usable" width of 40" after shrinkage and trimming selvages. Actual usable width will probably vary slightly from fabric to fabric. Our recommended yardage lengths should be adequate for occasional re-squaring of fabric when many cuts are required.

preparing fabrics

We recommend that all fabrics except felt be washed, dried, and pressed before cutting. Bright and dark colors, which may run, should always be washed before cutting. After washing and drying fabric, fold lengthwise with wrong sides together and matching selvages.

rotary cutting

- Place fabric on work surface with fold closest to you.
- Cut all strips from the selvage-to-selvage width of the fabric unless otherwise indicated in project instructions.
- Square left edge of fabric using rotary cutter and rulers (**Figs. 1 - 2**).

Fig. 1

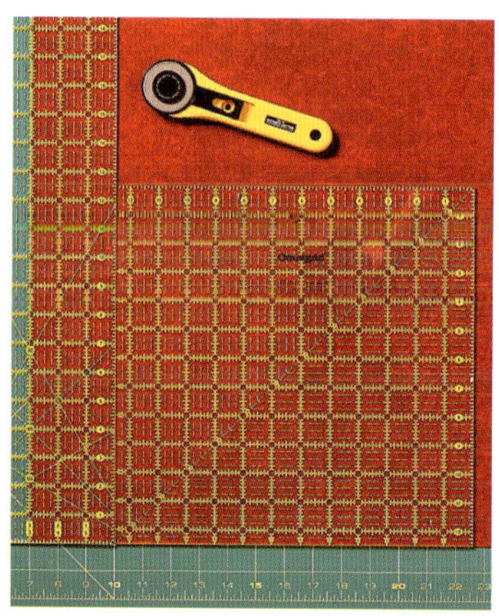

Fig. 2

- To cut each strip required for a project, place ruler over cut edge of fabric, aligning desired marking on ruler with cut edge; make cut (**Fig. 3**).

Fig. 3

- When cutting several strips from a single piece of fabric, it is important to make sure that cuts remain at a perfect right angle to the fold; square fabric as needed.

sewing

Precise cutting, followed by accurate sewing, will ensure that all the pieces of the project fit together well.

- Set sewing machine stitch length for approximately 11 stitches per inch.
- Use neutral-colored general-purpose sewing thread in needle and in bobbin.
- An accurate seam allowance is *essential*.
- When sewing, place pieces right sides together and match raw edges unless otherwise indicated; pin if necessary.

pressing

- Use steam iron set on "Cotton" for all pressing.
- Press after sewing each seam.
- Seam allowances are almost always pressed to one side, usually toward the darker fabric. However, to reduce bulk it may occasionally be necessary to press seam allowances toward the lighter fabric or even to press them open.
- To prevent dark fabric seam allowance from showing through light fabric, trim darker seam allowance slightly narrower than lighter seam allowance.

appliqué

template cutting

1. To make a template from a pattern, use a permanent fine-point pen and a ruler to carefully trace pattern onto template plastic. Cut out template along drawn line. Check template against original pattern for accuracy.
2. Place template on **right** side of appliqué fabric. Lightly draw around template with pencil, leaving at least $^1/_2$" between shapes. Repeat for number of shapes specified in project instructions.
3. Cut out shapes $^1/_4$" outside drawn line.

needle-turn appliqué

Using a needle to turn under seam allowance while blindstitching appliqué to background fabric is called "needle-turn appliqué."

1. Thread a sharps needle with a single strand of general-purpose sewing thread that matches appliqué; knot one end.
2. Begin blindstitching on as straight an edge as possible, turning a small section of seam allowance to wrong side with needle, concealing drawn line (**Fig. 4**).

Fig. 4

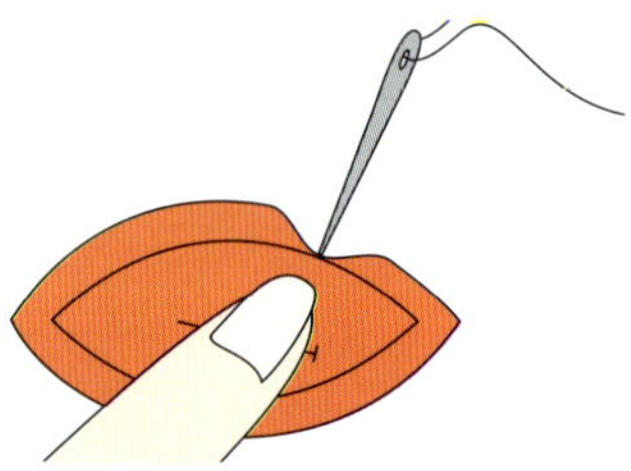

3. To stitch outward points, stitch to 1/2" from point (**Fig. 5**). Turn seam allowance under at point (**Fig. 6**); then turn remainder of seam allowance between stitching and point. Stitch to point, taking two or three stitches at top of point to secure. Turn under small amount of seam allowance past point and resume stitching.

Fig. 5

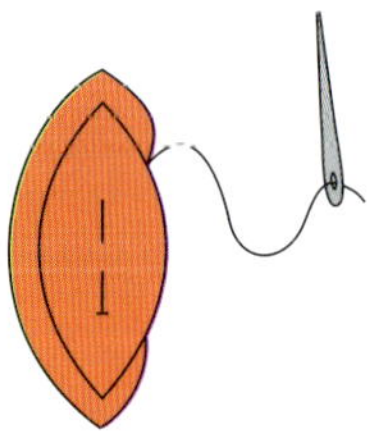

Fig. 6

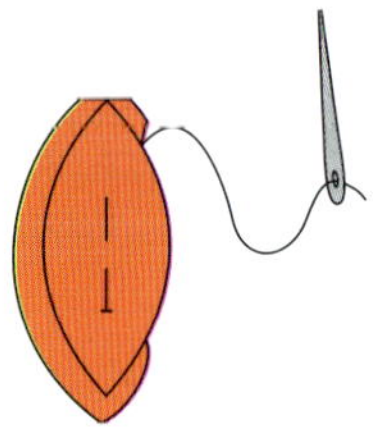

4. To stitch inward points, stitch to 1/2" from point (**Fig. 7**). Clip to but not through seam allowance at point (**Fig. 8**). Turn seam allowance under between stitching and point. Stitch to point, taking two or three stitches at point to secure. Turn under small amount of seam allowance past point and resume stitching.

Fig. 7

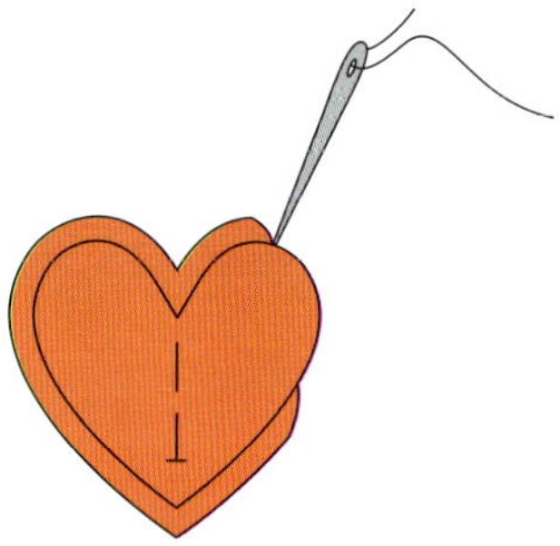

Fig. 8

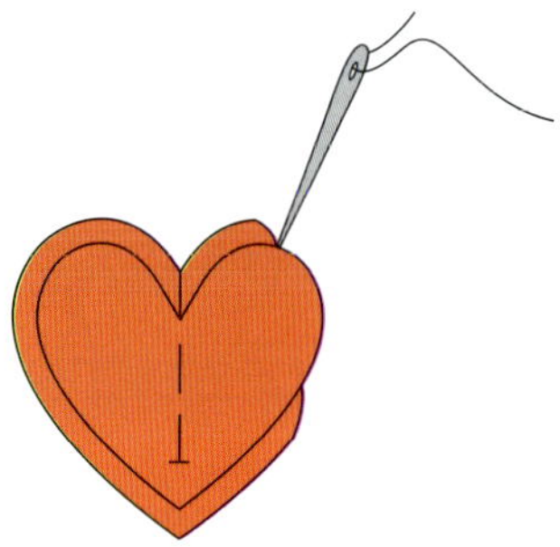

preparing fusible appliqués

White or light-colored fabrics may need to be lined with fusible interfacing before applying fusible web to prevent darker fabrics from showing through.

1. Place paper-backed fusible web, paper side up, over appliqué pattern. Trace pattern onto paper side of web with pencil as many times as indicated in project instructions for a single fabric.

2. Follow manufacturer's instructions to fuse traced patterns to wrong side of fabrics. Do not remove paper backing.
3. Use scissors to cut out appliqué pieces along traced lines. Remove paper backing from all pieces.

satin stitch appliqué

A satin stitch is a smooth line of zigzag stitching that covers the exposed raw edges of appliqué pieces fused to a background.

1. Pin stabilizer, such as paper or any of the commercially available products, on wrong side of background fabric before stitching appliqués in place.
2. Thread sewing machine with general-purpose thread; use general-purpose thread that matches background fabric in bobbin.
3. Set sewing machine for a medium (approximately 1/8") zigzag stitch and a short to medium stitch length. ***(Note:** Smaller projects may require a narrower stitch.)* Slightly loosening the top tension may yield a smoother stitch.
4. Begin by stitching two or three stitches in place (drop feed dogs or set stitch length at 0) to anchor thread. Most of the Satin Stitch should be on the appliqué with the right edge of the stitch falling at the outside edge of the appliqué. Stitch over all exposed raw edges of appliqué pieces.
5. (***Note:*** Dots on **Figs. 9 – 14** indicate where to leave needle in fabric when pivoting.) For outside corners, stitch just past corner, stopping with needle in background fabric (**Fig. 9**). Raise presser foot. Pivot project, lower presser foot, and stitch adjacent side (**Fig. 10**).

Fig. 9

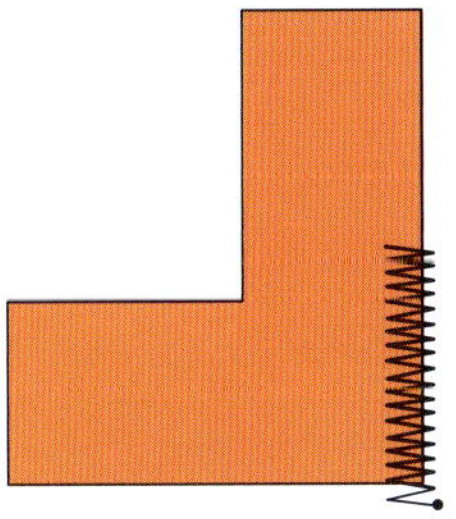

Fig. 10

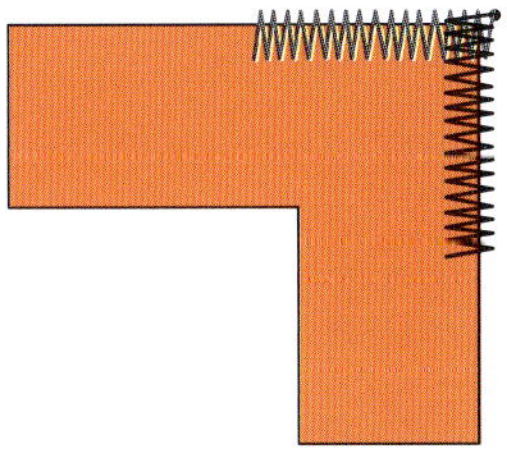

6. For inside corners, stitch just past corner, stopping with needle in appliqué fabric (**Fig. 11**). Raise presser foot. Pivot project, lower presser foot, and stitch adjacent side (**Fig. 12**).

Fig. 11

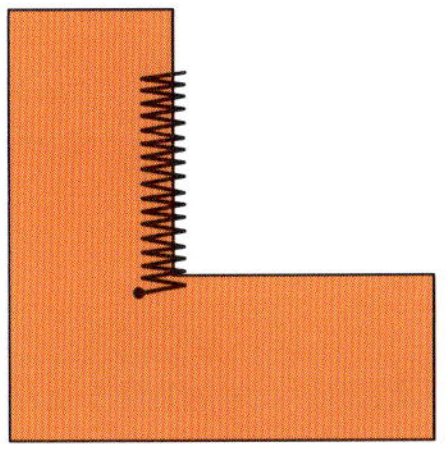

Fig. 12

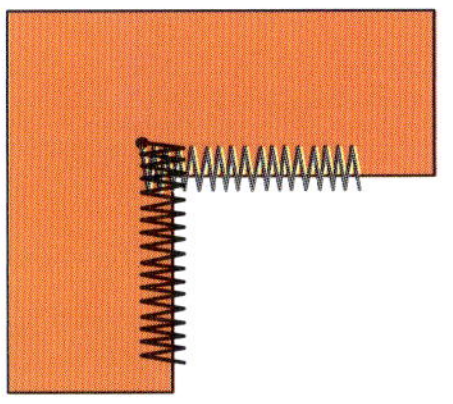

7. When stitching outside curves, stop with needle in background fabric. Raise presser foot and pivot project as needed. Lower presser foot and continue stitching, pivoting as often as necessary to follow curve (**Fig. 13**).

Fig. 13

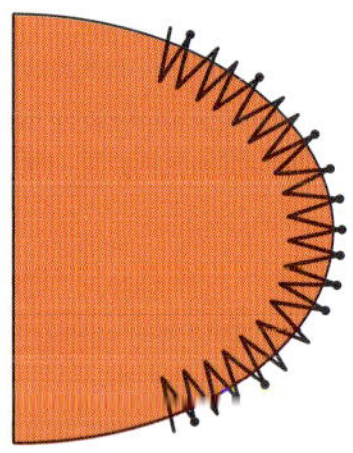

8. When stitching inside curves, stop with needle in appliqué fabric. Raise presser foot and pivot project as needed. Lower presser foot and continue stitching, pivoting as often as necessary to follow curve (**Fig. 14**).

Fig. 14

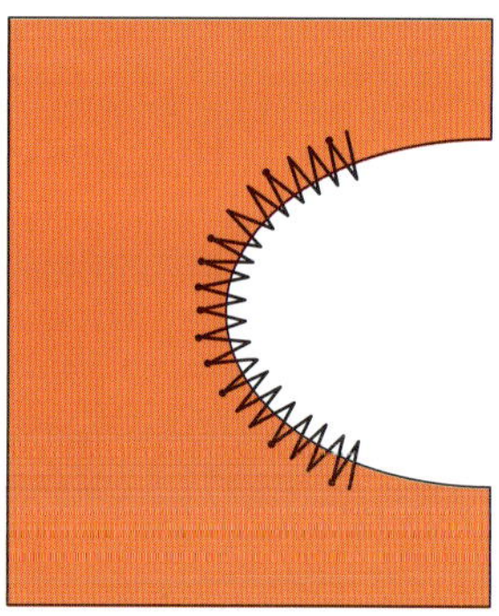

9. Do not backstitch at end of stitching. Pull threads to wrong side of background fabric; knot thread and trim ends.
10. Carefully tear away stabilizer.

quilting

*Quilting holds the three layers (top, batting, and backing) of the quilt together and can be done by hand or machine. Because marking, layering, and quilting are interrelated and may be done in different orders depending on circumstances, please read entire **Quilting** section, pages 40 – 43, before beginning project.*

types of quilting designs

in the ditch quilting

Quilting along seamlines or along edges of appliquéd pieces is called "in the ditch" quilting. This type of quilting should be done on side **opposite** seam allowance and does not have to be marked.

outline quilting

Quilting a consistent distance, usually 1/4", from seam or appliqué is called "outline" quilting. Outline quilting may be marked, or 1/4" masking tape may be placed along seamlines for quilting guide. (Do not leave tape on quilt longer than necessary, since it may leave an adhesive residue.)

echo quilting

Quilting that follows the outline of an appliquéd or pieced design with two or more parallel lines is called "echo" quilting. This type of quilting does not need to be marked.

meandering quilting

Quilting in random curved lines and swirls is called "meandering" quilting. Quilting lines should not cross or touch each other. This type of quilting does not need to be marked.

marking quilting lines

Quilting lines may be marked using fabric marking pencils, chalk markers, water- or air-soluble pens, or lead pencils.

Simple quilting designs may be marked with chalk or chalk pencil after basting. A small area may be marked, then quilted, before moving to next area to be marked. Intricate designs should be marked before basting using a more durable marker.

Caution: Pressing may permanently set some marks. **Test** different markers **on scrap fabric** to find one that marks clearly and can be thoroughly removed.

A wide variety of pre-cut quilting stencils, as well as entire books of quilting patterns, are available. Using a stencil makes it easier to mark intricate or repetitive designs.

To make a stencil from a pattern, center template plastic over pattern and use a permanent marker to trace pattern onto plastic. Use a craft knife with single or double blade to cut channels along traced lines (**Fig. 15**).

Fig. 15

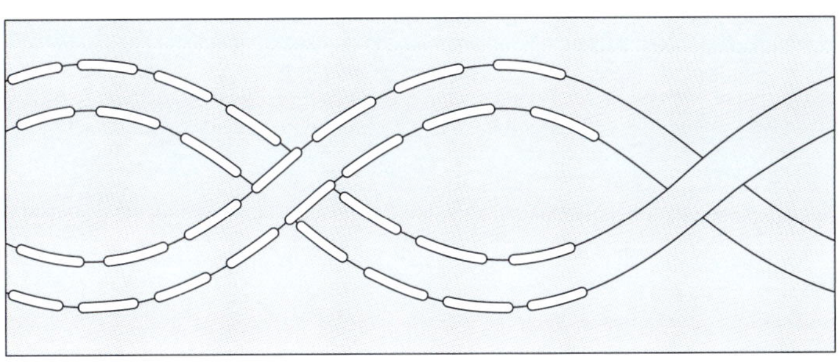

preparing the backing

To allow for slight shifting of quilt top during quilting, backing should be approximately 4" larger on all sides. Yardage requirements listed for quilt backings are calculated for 43"/44"w fabric. To piece a backing using 43"/44"w fabric, use the following instructions.

1. Measure length and width of quilt top; add 8" to each measurement.
2. Cut backing fabric into two lengths slightly longer than determined *length* measurement. *(**Note:** Sometimes less fabric yardage may be required if the backing is pieced horizontally. Divide determined length measurement by 40" to determine how many widths will be needed. Cut required number of widths the determined width measurement.)* Trim selvages. Place lengths with right sides facing and sew long edges together, forming a tube (**Fig. 16**). Match seams and press along one fold (**Fig. 17**). Cut along pressed fold to form single piece (**Fig. 18**).

Fig. 16

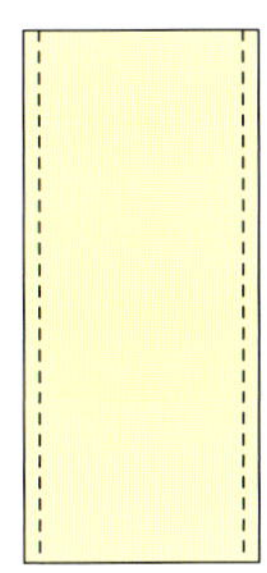

Fig. 17

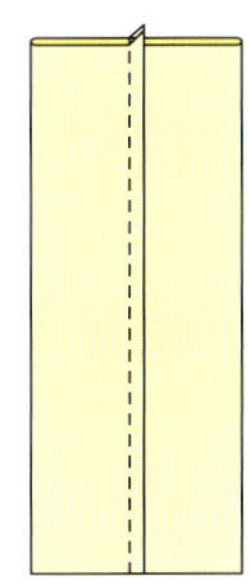

Fig. 18

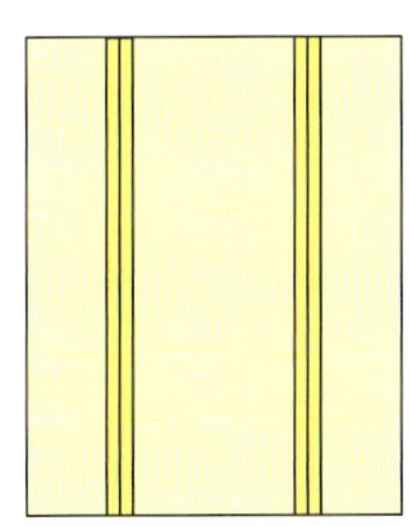

3. Trim backing to size determined in Step 1; press seam allowances open.

choosing the batting

The appropriate batting will make quilting easier. For fine hand quilting, choose low-loft batting. All cotton or cotton/polyester blend battings work well for machine quilting because the cotton helps "grip" quilt layers. If quilt is to be tied, a high-loft batting, sometimes called extra-loft or fat batting, may be used to make quilt "fluffy."

Types of batting include cotton, polyester, wool, cotton/polyester blend, cotton/wool blend, and silk.

When selecting batting, refer to package labels for characteristics and care instructions.

assembling the quilt

1. Examine wrong side of quilt top closely; trim any seam allowances and clip any threads that may show through front of the quilt. Press quilt top, being careful not to "set" any marked quilting lines.
2. Place backing **wrong** side up on flat surface. Use masking tape to tape edges of backing to surface. Place batting on top of backing fabric. Smooth batting gently, being careful not to stretch or tear. Center quilt top *right* side up on batting.
3. Use 1" rustproof safety pins to "pin-baste" all layers together, spacing pins approximately 4" apart. Begin at center and work toward outer edges to secure all layers. If possible, place pins away from areas that will be quilted, although pins may be removed as needed when quilting.

machine quilting methods

Use general-purpose thread in bobbin. Do not use quilting thread. Thread the needle of machine with general-purpose thread or transparent monofilament thread to make quilting blend with quilt top fabrics. Use decorative thread, such as a metallic or contrasting-color general-purpose thread, to make quilting lines stand out more.

straight-line quilting

The term "straight-line" is somewhat deceptive, since curves (especially gentle ones) as well as straight lines can be stitched with this technique.

1. Set stitch length for six to ten stitches per inch and attach walking foot to sewing machine.
2. Determine which section of quilt will have longest continuous quilting line, oftentimes area from center top to center bottom. Roll up and secure each edge of quilt to help reduce the bulk, keeping fabrics smooth. Smaller projects may not need to be rolled.
3. Begin stitching on longest quilting line, using very short stitches for the first 1/4" to "lock" quilting. Stitch across project, using one hand on each side of walking foot to slightly spread fabric and to guide fabric through machine. Lock stitches at end of quilting line.
4. Continue machine quilting, stitching longer quilting lines first to stabilize quilt before moving on to other areas.

free-motion quilting

Free-motion quilting may be free form or may follow a marked pattern.

1. Attach darning foot to sewing machine and lower or cover feed dogs.
2. Position quilt under darning foot; lower foot. Holding top thread, take a stitch and pull bobbin thread to top of quilt. To "lock" beginning of quilting line, hold top and bobbin threads while making three to five stitches in place.
3. Use one hand on each side of darning foot to slightly spread fabric and to move fabric through the machine. Even stitch length is achieved by using smooth, flowing hand motion and steady machine speed. Slow machine speed and fast hand movement will create long stitches. Fast machine speed and slow hand movement will create short stitches. Move quilt sideways, back and forth, in a circular motion, or in a random motion to create desired designs; do not rotate quilt. Lock stitches at end of each quilting line.

making a hanging sleeve

Attaching a hanging sleeve to back of wall hanging or quilt before the binding is added allows project to be displayed on wall.

1. Measure width of quilt top edge and subtract 1". Cut piece of fabric 7"w by determined measurement.
2. Press short edges of fabric piece 1/4" to wrong side; press edges 1/4" to wrong side again and machine stitch in place.
3. Matching wrong sides, fold piece in half lengthwise to form tube.
4. Match raw edges and stitch hanging sleeve to center top edge on back of quilt.
5. Finish binding quilt, treating hanging sleeve as part of backing.
6. Blindstitch bottom of hanging sleeve to backing, taking care not to stitch through to front of quilt.

binding

making straight-grain binding

1. Cut lengthwise or crosswise strips of binding fabric the determined length and width called for in project instructions.
2. Using a diagonal seam (**Fig. 19**), sew binding strips together end to end.

Fig. 19

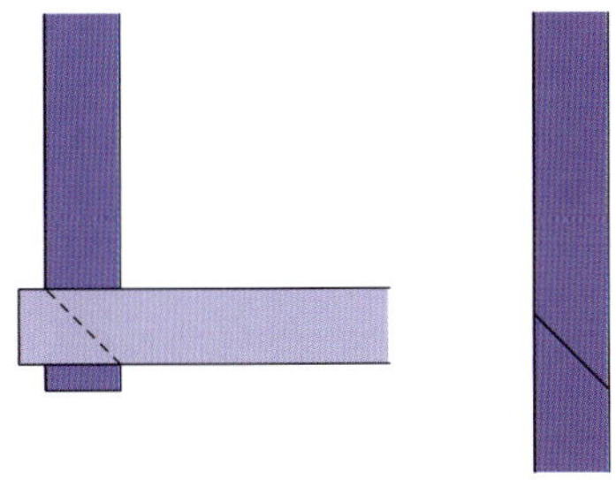

3. Matching wrong sides and raw edges, press strip(s) in half lengthwise to complete binding.

attaching binding with mitered corners

For a quick and easy finish when attaching binding, sew your binding to the back of the quilt and then stitch it in place on the front of the quilt, eliminating all hand stitching.

1. Using a narrow zigzag, stitch around quilt close to the raw edges (**Fig. 20**). Trim backing and batting even with edges of quilt top.

Fig. 20

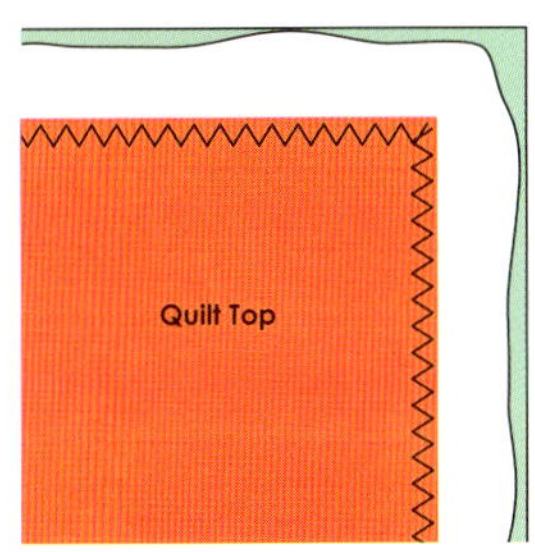

2. Beginning with one end near center on bottom edge of quilt, lay binding around quilt to make sure that seams in binding will not end up at a corner. Adjust placement if necessary. Matching raw edges of binding to raw edge of **quilt back**, pin binding to back of quilt along one edge.
3. When you reach first corner, mark 1/4" from corner of quilt back (**Fig. 21**).

Fig. 21

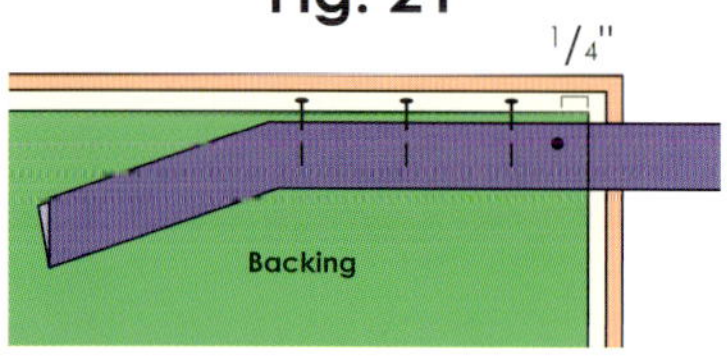

4. Beginning approximately 10" from end of binding and using 1/4" seam allowance, sew binding to quilt, backstitching at beginning of stitching and at mark (**Fig. 22**). Lift needle out of fabric and clip thread.

Fig. 22

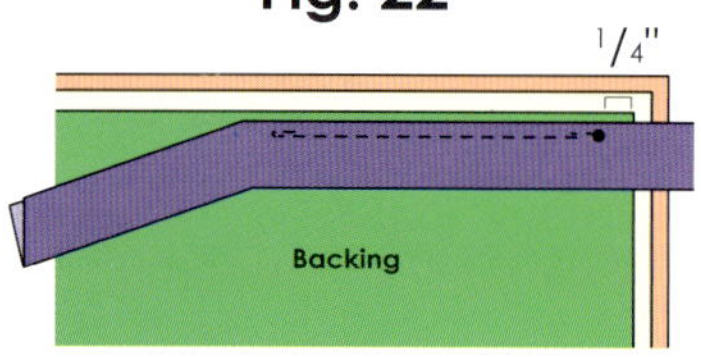

5. Fold binding as shown in **Figs. 23 – 24** and pin binding to adjacent side, matching raw edges. When you've reached the next corner, mark 1/4" from edge of quilt back.

Fig. 23

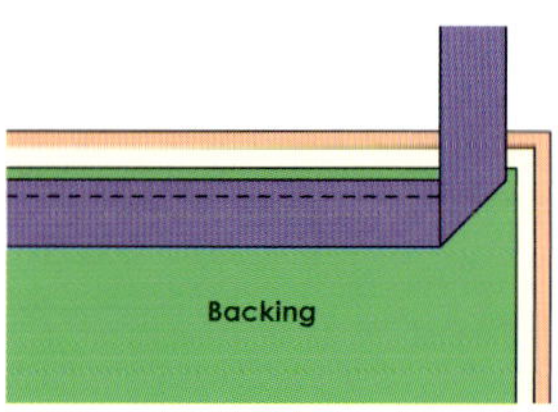

Fig. 24

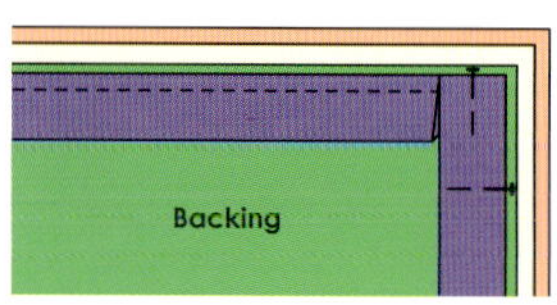

6. Backstitching at edge of quilt back, sew pinned binding to quilt (**Fig. 25**); backstitch at the next mark. Lift needle out of fabric and clip thread.

Fig. 25

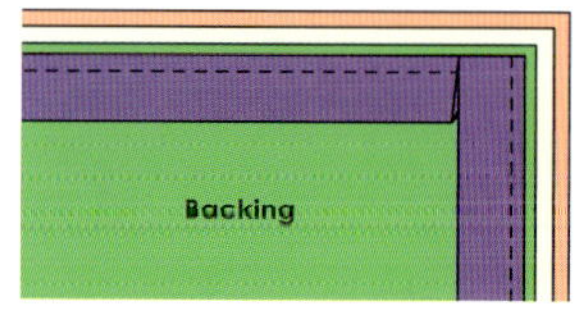

7. Continue sewing binding to quilt, stopping approximately 10" from starting point (**Fig. 26**).

Fig. 26

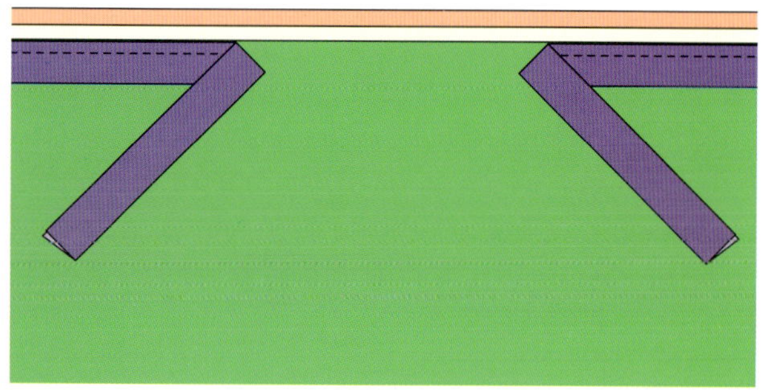

8. Bring beginning and end of binding to center of opening and fold each end back, leaving a 1/4" space between folds (**Fig. 27**). Finger press folds.

Fig. 27

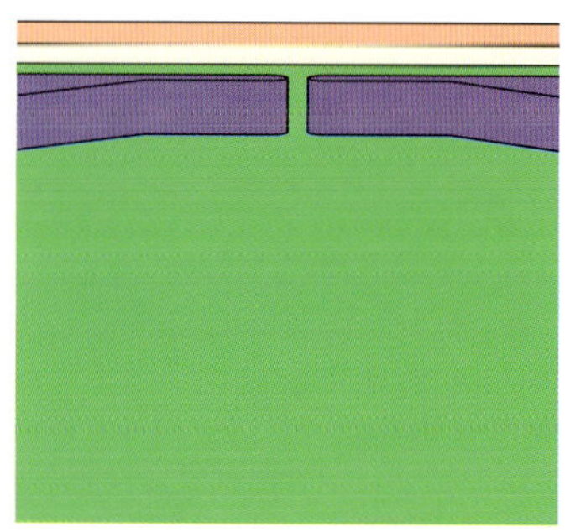

9. Unfold ends of binding and draw a line across wrong side in finger-pressed crease. Draw a line through the lengthwise pressed fold of binding at the same spot to create a cross mark. With edge of ruler at cross mark, line up 45° angle marking on ruler with one long side of binding. Draw a diagonal line from edge to edge. Repeat on remaining end, making sure that the two diagonal lines are angled the same way (**Fig. 28**).

Fig. 28

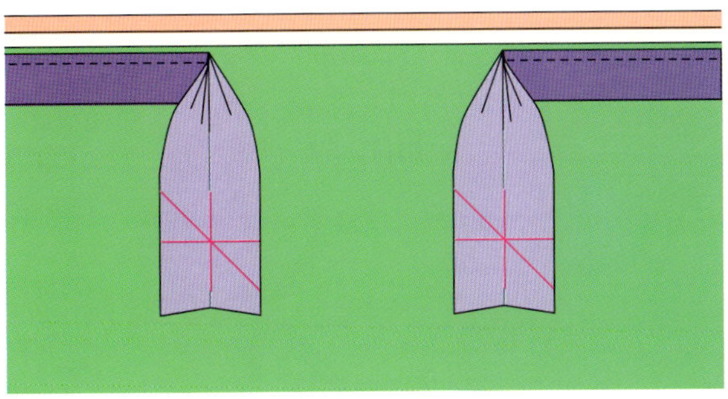

10. Matching right sides and diagonal lines, pin binding ends together a right angles (**Fig. 29**).

Fig. 29

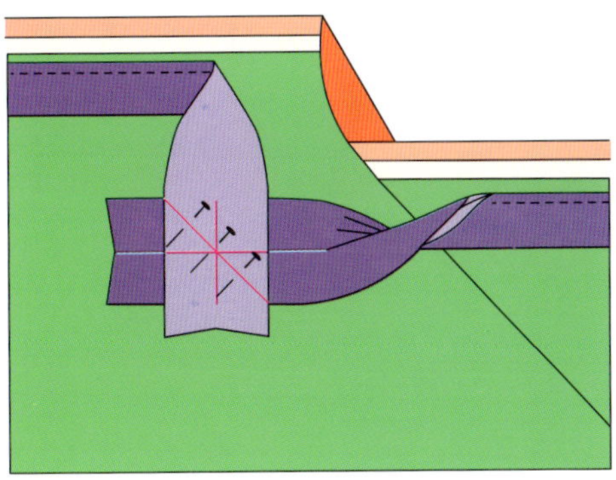

11. Machine stitch along diagonal line (**Fig. 30**), removing pins as you stitch.

Fig. 30

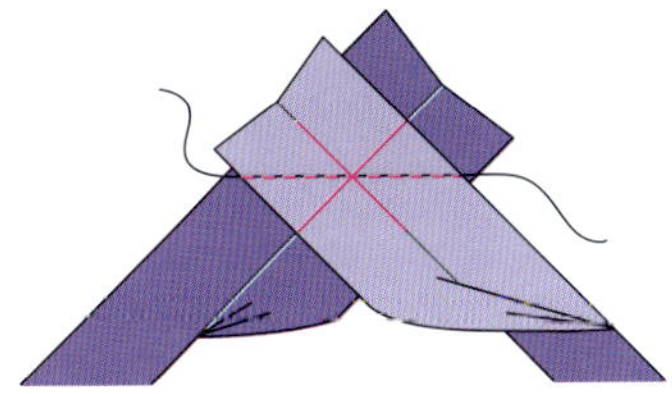

12. Lay binding against quilt to double check that it is correct length.
13. Trim binding ends, leaving 1/4" seam allowance; press seam open. Stitch binding to quilt.
14. On one edge of quilt, fold binding over to quilt front and pin pressed edge in place, covering stitching line (**Fig. 31**). On adjacent side, fold binding over, forming a mitered corner (**Fig. 32**). Repeat to pin remainder of binding in place.

Fig. 31

Fig. 32

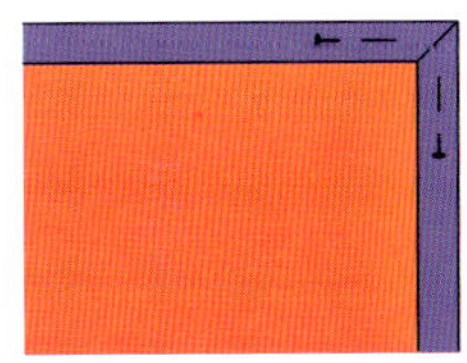

15. Topstitch binding to quilt top.

transferring embroidery patterns

1. Trace the pattern onto tissue paper and pin it to the fabric.
2. Embroider the design, stitching through the tissue paper.
3. Tear away the tissue paper.

hand stitches

back stitch

Come up at 1, go down at 2, and come up at 3 (**Fig. 33**). Length of stitches may be varied as desired.

Fig. 33

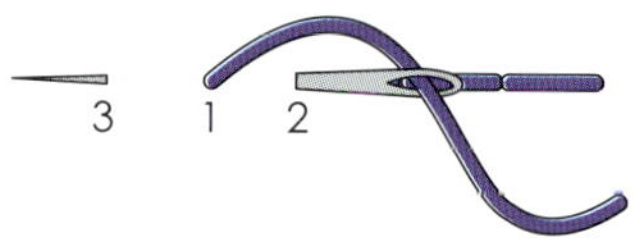

blind stitch

Come up at 1, go down at 2, and come up at 3 (**Fig. 34**). Length of stitches may be varied as desired.

Fig. 34

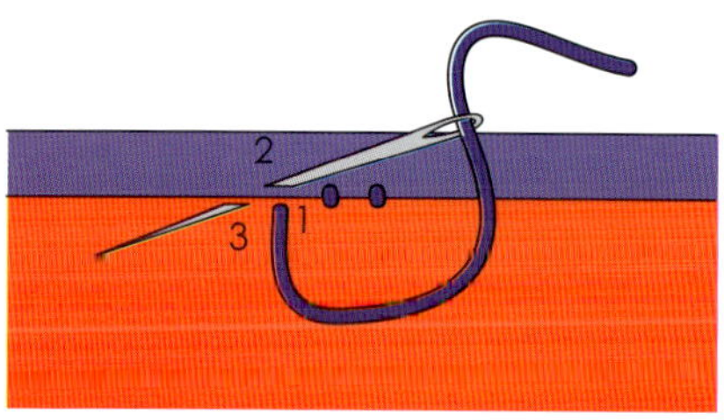

running stitch

The running stitch consists of a series of straight stitches with the stitch length equal to the space between stitches. Come up at 1, go down at 2, and come up at 3 (**Fig. 35**).

Fig. 35

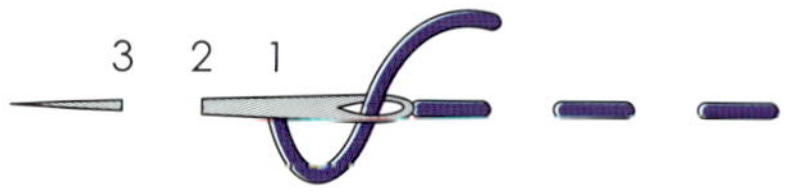

straight stitch

Come up at 1 and go down at 2 (**Fig. 36**). Length of stitches may be varied as desired.

Fig. 36

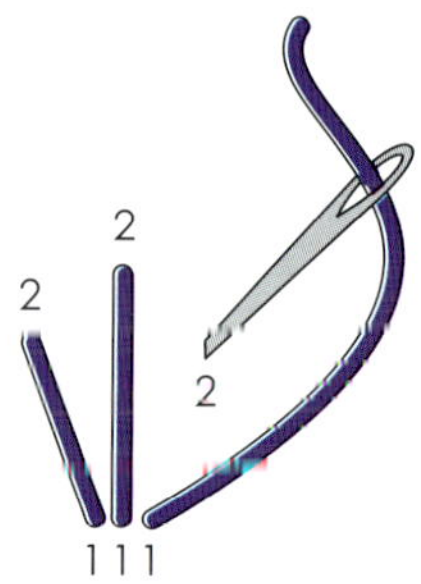

metric conversion chart

Inches x 2.54 = centimeters (cm)
Inches x 25.4 = millimeters (mm)
Inches x .0254 = meters (m)

Yards x .9144 = meters (m)
Yards x 91.44 = centimeters (cm)
Centimeters x .3937 = inches (")
Meters x 1.0936 = yards (yd)

1/8"	3.2 mm	0.32 cm	1/8 yard	11.43 cm	0.11 m
1/4"	6.35 mm	0.635 cm	1/4 yard	22.86 cm	0.23 m
3/8"	9.5 mm	0.95 cm	3/8 yard	34.29 cm	0.34 m
1/2"	12.7 mm	1.27 cm	1/2 yard	45.72 cm	0.46 m
5/8"	15.9 mm	1.59 cm	5/8 yard	57.15 cm	0.57 m
3/4"	19.1 mm	1.91 cm	3/4 yard	68.58 cm	0.69 m
7/8"	22.2 mm	2.22 cm	7/8 yard	80 cm	0.8 m
1 "	25.4 mm	2.54 cm	1 yard	91.44 cm	0.91 m

production team

senior technical writer **Lisa Lancaster** • production assistant **Jean Lewis**
editorial writer **Susan Johnson** • graphic designer **Angela Ormsby Stark**
graphic artist **Jacob Casleton** • photographer **Ken West**
photography stylist **Sondra Daniel**

meet the designer

Getting to know Linda Lum DeBono

New things are always going on in Linda Lum DeBono's world. Currently, the designer is launching a Web site, sending her youngest son to first grade ("I'm proud and sad at the same time," says Linda), and looking forward to seeing her latest color-charged fabric line from Henry Glass Fabrics.

As Linda says, "I'm always looking for the next thing in fashion. The best look is one that expresses what's hot without going over the top."

View Linda's latest fabrics and read her inspiration journal at www.lindalumdebono.com.

Want more Modern Crafter designs? You can create cool urban décor and chic baby fashions in a flash with #4427 *Home Stuff* and #4426 *Tot Stuff*. Get your copies at www.leisurearts.com.